Century

ing

Typography

Virginia Brook Publishing · Windsor

A *Qfax* Guide

Published by Virginia Brook Publishing

PO Box 1226 · Windsor · Berks ·SL4 5DN

First Impression · 1991

Copyright © 1991 Virginia Brook Publishing

ISBN 1 873547 00 5

This book was designed and produced
by Virginia Brook Publishing.

Printed in England by PrintWest · London

Contents

Introduction

This little book about typography is written for desktop publishers embarking on the use of type for the first time, and for those wanting to know more about using type. It will also be of interest to any consumer or specifier of type who wants to find out more about this fascinating subject.

Desktop publishing has brought more people into contact with type as users than ever before. It is much more than advanced word-processing (nonetheless many of the techniques described here are applicable to word-processing as well) and provides facilities for type manipulation that were previously available only to a privileged few.

Like many specialist disciplines, it has an arcane language all its own. Some of the terms used today would still be familiar to Gutenberg or Caxton. The language can, at first, appear bewilderingly complex. As with many things, lack of information makes it so.

I strongly believe that one of the main reasons people find DTP software difficult is because they are not familiar with the language of the typographer. I also believe that even a basic grounding in typography will pay enormous dividends in terms of the quality of documents produced.

This book was written to present and explain in a practical way the language of typography. All the principles and techniques described here are relevant to desktop publishing and can be applied with familiar software packages such as Ventura, PageMaker, QuarkXpress, and Interleaf to name but a few.

As ornate and beautiful as type can be, its use is as much science as art. Type was not invented for decoration but for communication. As a user of type your job and the function of the type you use is to present any written message to the reader in the most legible form. It is a happy coincidence that, in many cases, the most aesthetically pleasing layout happens to be the most legible.

The book is designed to be used as a desktop reference. Not all desktop publishers use their software every day and you may forget things between times. Keep this book handy as a reminder that you can refer to whenever required.

The study of type and typography can be very rewarding on a personal and a professional level. Users of desktop publishing are very fortunate in having at their disposal facilities for experimenting with type for minimal cost (other than the initial outlay!).

I hope that this book will be just the starting point for your typographical studies. I hope too that it will encourage you to extend your knowledge of the software that you use, and to implement some of the more sophisticated functions that it provides.

A Note on Copy

My interest in typography grew out of my interest (and employment) in writing. They deserve the best of each other.

I would strongly urge an exponent of either discipline to learn something of the other. Good copy deserves good typography: and vice versa. In my work I see many examples of tasteful design that are, for me, ruined by poor copy.

It seems at times as if the content has somehow become secondary to the overall aesthetic appeal of the page. I find this perverse; who is influenced or entertained solely by good design?

The purpose of page design is not to present a random assemblage of words and phrases in an appealing manner. It is to invite a reader, whose initial interest may only be casual, into a carefully composed web of words that will lead him or her down a road to a point where some sort of response or recognition is stimulated.

There are of course other psychological factors that come into play, and these are not the subject of this book. This book is about communicating ideas in print and this cannot be divorced from the use of the words as language as distinct from art.

If you are working alone, don't just blindly process text and pictures. They are your raw materials. Read and check for brevity and precision. Be ruthless with punctuation and grammar. If you are allowed, cut out unnecessary and outmoded phrases, or vague and imprecise words.

If you are part of team interact with the other 'players'. Find out what a publication is designed to do. Be a contributor, and let the function determine the form.

A Brief History of Typography

> *"...the application and implication of new techniques is likely to be better understood by those who have an understanding of the events and results of the past than by those who are ignorant of what has gone before."*

The history of of typography makes a fascinating study in itself. It covers a period of almost 2000 years and crosses the world from the Orient to Renaissance Europe, and takes in The Industrial Revolution in Great Britain.

The history of the development and use of type is almost inseparable from the history of the printing and publishing industry. Not until the eighteenth century did typefounding break from printing as a totally separate craft and even then printers were to be actively concerned with typeface design.

Early Days

It is impossible to say who 'invented' printing but block printing was known in China in the ninth century and was probably practiced earlier. The invention of paper was reported to the Chinese emperor Ts'ai Lun in AD 105. Paper was being made in Europe about AD 1150. Italy was making paper in 1270 but not until 1494, with the opening of John Tate's mill, was paper made in England.

Separate type characters appeared in China during the period 1041-1049. In the thirteenth century metal type was used in the Far East for the first time and spread widely in the region. It eventually died out because it was not suited to ideographic characters and the requirements of calligraphers.

During the fourteenth century, block books and prints were seen in increasing numbers but the introduction of movable type, generally credited to Johannes Gutenberg, sparked off an era of rapid development in the printing industry.

Gutenberg may have been a great inventor but he does not appear to have been a successful businessman. He borrowed heavily to finance his invention and the printing of the Gutenberg bible. His financier, a wealthy goldsmith, was eventually forced to sue Gutenberg to recover his money. The legal action was successful and Gutenberg was forced to withdraw from his press, leaving his colleague Peter Schoffer and his backer, Johannes Fust, to complete the now famous 42-line bible.

The high standard achieved by Gutenberg and his contemporaries gave rise to a rapid expansion of the art of printing. The European Renaissance hastened the expansion by creating a demand for books to satisfy the burgeoning interest in and demand for literature.

The Development of Printing in Europe

If we look first at Italy, Venice offers the greatest interest in the development of printing. The first notable figure was Nicolas Jenson, who was sent to Mainz to learn the invention of printing by Charles VII of France. He never made it home but settled instead in Venice and set up a press and cut a type that has become famous as a model for the Venetian Group of typefaces.

The next Venetian printer was also a publisher. Aldus Manutius founded his press in 1488. His work as a scholar and teacher had created an interest in producing good text books and he is best remembered for his work in printing the works of Aristotle. Aldus is remembered for his preservation of many of the classics and for his outstanding pioneer work in the art of book printing.

Around 1498 Aldus published *De Aetna* for Pietro Bembo. For this work he commissioned his punch cutter, Francesco Griffo of Bologna, to cut a new roman letter which became the model for a type group now called Old Face. To enable Aldus to publish books of a more manageable size Francesco Griffo also cut a sloping letter that we now know as italic.

While printing was developing in Italy there was much activity in Germany, especially in the towns of Bamberg,

Strassburg, and Cologne. Printing in Bamberg was started by Albert Pfister who is thought to be the first to use woodcuts to illustrate his books.

Between 1471 and 1472 it was a Cologne-based printer Ulrich Zell who taught printing to William Caxton. While a member of the household of the Duchess of Burgundy, Caxton had begun to translate the *History of Troy* from the French. Caxton visited Cologne to learn the new craft and returned to his base in Bruges to establish a press where he printed his translation: the first book in English.

Caxton came to England in 1476 and set up a press near Westminster Abbey. He published only in English and did not regard Greek and Latin as commercially viable for the home market. He was an able editor and translator and served English literature by printing such books as Chaucer's *Canterbury Tales* and Malory's *Morte d'Arthur*.

After Caxton's death in 1491 his foreman moved the press to the City of London where there were several other printers already established. By the middle of the sixteenth century there was a large number of printers in and near London.

Printing was introduced to France around 1470, with the first presses being established at the Sorbonne. One of the most important figures at the time was Antoine Verard who, in a very active career, helped to give France a lead in book production.

Another famous name in French printing was that of the Estienne family. Robert Estienne and his son Henri enjoyed the support of Francois I of France and made many important contributions to printing.

It was the Estienne family who obtained the services of punch cutter Claude Garamond, the most famous of French type designers. Garamond died in poverty but his types were used long after his death.

Although unsupported by evidence, it is said that it was a Dutchman, Laurens Janszoon Coster, who invented printing from movable type and that on his death the idea was taken to Mainz by one of his workmen. True or not, the Low Countries did make an important contribution to the development of printing.

Christopher Plantin was the most famous publisher in the Low Countries. He became involved in printing by chance after an accident curtailed his career as a book-binder. In 1569 he was appointed printer to the King and began his most famous work: a polyglot Bible in four languages occupying four volumes. Plantin was later to be associated with the Elzevir family in Leyden following the collapse of his business owing to the war with Spain.

Louis Elzevir set up as a bookseller in 1580 and established a famous family publishing house that was continued by his six sons. The most successful Elzevir publications were small volumes remarkable for their clarity.

The types used by the family were cut by Christopher van Dyck. The combined efforts of the Elzevir family and Plantin ensured that Holland largely monopolised sixteenth-century type trade.

The Eighteenth Century

By the beginning of the eighteenth century, printing had become an important industry. Despite this progress machinery had progressed little beyond the modified 'wine-presses' of the fifteenth century. Some notable figures did, however, arise.

Among these was an Englishman, William Caslon, who served as an apprentice engraver then set up business in London in 1716. With financial backing, Caslon established a typefoundry which proved so successful that he was able to erode the monopoly enjoyed by the Dutch.

Around 1734 Caslon issued a type specimen sheet showing his now celebrated Caslon Old Face in fourteen sizes. This face is reckoned to be one of the most legible ever designed. (Caslon's business continued for three generations after his death with the firm eventually being absorbed in 1937.)

At this time, a Scotsman named William Ged invented a process for casting type and printing from a plate. The invention was not well received by established printers and after a few unsuccessful demonstrations in London Ged returned to Scotland where he died before he could further his invention.

Ged was not the only Scottish innovator of influence. Glasgow rose to fame as a printing centre and the Foulis brothers, while printers to the university, achieved an extremely high standard of printing and typographical accuracy.

One John Baskerville was also active during the eighteenth century and established his reputation with his edition of *Virgil* in 1757. In 1758 he was appointed Printer to Cambridge University and printed a folio bible in 1763.

Towards the end of the century John Bell arrived on the printing scene. He started a number of newspapers and completely revised newspaper typography. One of his papers — *The Morning Post* — lasted from 1772 until 1937 as a national daily.

In France the eighteenth century saw an important development in type design which gave rise to the 'romain du roi': a typeface specially designed for the Imprimerie Royale of Louis XIV. One Pierre Simon Fournier issued a range of types in the new style to which he gave the name 'modern' — a term still in use today.

Fournier has another claim to fame. In 1737 he introduced a system of uniform body sizes and his ideas were to lead to the

Point System of body measurement. The modern face also occupied the thinking of the Didot family. The efforts of this family and those of Fournier attracted the interest of Giambattista Bodoni.

Bodoni was born in Saluzzo in Italy and learned printing from his father. He has the reputation of being a perfectionist and it has been said that for him a book was solely a means of displaying good printing and type design.

Growing activity in printing was the keynote of the eighteenth century. In the previous century there was a evidence of declining typographical standards and this tendency became more marked as the eighteenth century drew to a close.

The Nineteenth Century

The nineteenth century was a period of considerable expansion in the printing industry — notable more for the quantity than the quality of its output. Rapid development was made possible by a combination of economic, scientific, political, and social factors.

Developments were recorded in both the printing and allied industries. Paper making became a mechanical rather than manual process and significant developments in press technology were at long last effected.

Frederich Koenig of Saxony came to England in 1806 after failing to raise capital for his printing machine. With the encouragement of Thomas Bensley he built a cylinder machine that was adopted by *The Times* in 1814 through the enthusiasm of James Walter. Walter thought the new press so revolutionary that he contrived to have it constructed and assembled in secret.

Developments in photography also provided the means for new printing techniques. The pioneer work of Meisenbach and of Louis and Max Levy enabled a 'screen' to be made from which it was possible to secure a half-tone negative. The first half-tone picture to be seen in the British Press appeared in the *Daily Graphic* in 1891.

Improvements made in methods of composition are assumed to have started with the invention of Dr William Church who devised a type assembling machine in 1822. This was followed by a number of attempts to mechanise composition.

In 1886 Ottmar Mergenthaler produced the first Linotype machine which was installed in the office of the *New York Tribune*. The first Linotype machine in Britain arrived in 1901.

Increased commercial activity during the period meant increased advertising. This gave rise to the style of composition known as 'display setting'. To service this discipline new 'display' types were developed, leading to the introduction of new type groups such as Sans and Grotesque. Classic faces also made a comeback. William Pickering and Charles Whittingham, who started their association in 1830, revived in 1840 the Old Face type designed by Caslon.

The Twentieth Century

The twentieth century will be remembered for increasing automation and computerisation of printing and publishing. It will also be remembered for something of a renaissance in typographical standards.

Frederick Goudy founded the Village Press in 1903 and, during his remarkable career, this industrious American was responsible for introducing some hundred and sixteen founts of type. Jacob Erbar designed the type that bears his name, and the type designed by Edward Johnston in 1916 marked the rise of sans as a popular design.

Johnston was a member of the Imprint Group formed to study and produce fine bookwork. The group published its own magazine *Imprint* which featured a type designed by Meynell and Mason, subsequently issued by Monotype in 1913. This face was regarded as the first acceptable book face since the Old Face of Caslon's time.

Imprint type marked a classic revival and Monotype secured the services of Stanley Morison to direct their research. It was he who created Times New Roman for the restyled *Times* of 1932. Among the first faces to be issued were Baskerville, Fournier, and Gill Sans.

In 1928, after visiting the Bauhaus in 1913, Tscichold published *The New Typography*. Three years before this work appeared, Tschichold went to Munich where he worked under Paul Renner who designed Futura, one of the many sans types issued in the fifteen years following the First War — a period of remarkable activity on the part of the German typefounders.

The various disciplines that comprise printing and publishing have all undergone considerable development during the twentieth century. The latter part of the century has seen a transition from hot metal typecasting machines to phototypesetters and now state of the art imagesetters capable of imaging complex pages of mixed text and graphics.

Desktop publishing is very much part of this development, and it is interesting to reflect on the parallels that exist with the rapid expansion in demand for published material witnessed during The Industrial Revolution. The new technology, far from leading to the 'paperless office' has led to further expansion in the provision of many types of published material.

Now, more than ever, type and the means for its manipulation are available to a large number of users, very few of whom have received even the most basic training in typography. And yet, today's software provides all the tools required to produce work of excellent typographical quality in the hands of a sympathetic user.

The words of W H Larken, written 30 years ago in his *Compositors Work in Printing*, apply very much to the present.

". . . it is easy for the technician to adopt a 'push-button mentality' in this age of 'push-button technique'. From reading printing history, it is evident that the industry has been enriched by the efforts of outstanding craftsmen to whom it owes the foundation of basic processes and principles . . . although the practices of the craftsmen have changed, his purpose has not and all forms of development are aimed at producing good printing which will be informative and attractive to the user . . ."

"There is still an unsurpassed pleasure in the possession of beautiful printing. Indeed, printing itself remains something of considerable significance; it is an art that attracts those who wish to think, and the application and implication of new techniques is likely to be better understood by He who has an understanding of the events and results of the past than by He who is ignorant of what has gone before."

Glossary

This glossary contains definitions for more than 100 commonly encountered typographical terms. Many of the terms are put into a practical context in the main body of the book.

A

Agate

A unit of vertical measurement of newspaper space. 14 agate lines equal one inch.

Art Paper

Coated paper with a glossy surface.

Ascender

The part of a letter that extends above the x-height of lower case letters as in b, d, h, k.

B

Bad Break

Incorrect word division, such as improper hyphenation not between syllables. Also, setting a hyphenated word on the first line of a page.
see also: HYPHENATION

Banner

The main headline running across the top of a page in newspapers or journals.

Baseline

An imaginary horizontal line on which the bottom of capital letters and lower case letters such as 'a' and 'x' appear to rest.

Binding Margin

Additional space left for binding on the inside edge of the page.

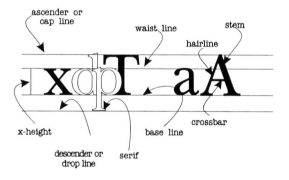

above: a diagram showing the parts and basic
dimensions of type.

Bleed

The printed area extending beyond the trimmed edge of a page. Also the extra width on artwork indicating that an illustration will bleed off the edge of the page: usually about 4mm in extent.

Body

The vertical area occupied by a character, including white space above and below.

Body Type

Type of 14 points or less used for continuous text, as distinct from headings or display type.

Bold, Boldface

Type with a conspicuously heavy, black appearance. Based on the same design as medium weight type of the same font.

Break

An interruption to the normal flow of text, e.g. from page to page or column to column.

Broadsheet

Large size newspaper format, printing on a full size sheet.

Bromide

Photo-sensitive paper that carries the image of type and line-art/graphics after setting. Always black on white.

Bullet

A typographical device used at the beginning of a line or paragraph to draw the reader's eye. Commonly used to separate vertically a list of items requiring special emphasis.

C

Camera-Ready Copy

Imageset or laser-printed output that can be used without further modification for conversion to lithographic plates by a reproduction ('repro') house.

see also: REPRODUCTION

Cap Height

The height of upper case letters measured from baseline to the top of a capital letter.

Caps

Abbreviation for capitals, i.e. type in upper case.

Caption

The heading of a page of type, or the large display letters at the top of an ad'. Usually 18 points or larger.

Chapter Drop

The measure of space from the chapter heading down to the first line of text.

Cicero

A unit of measurement used in the European system that is exactly 12 didot points (i.e. 4.52mm/0.178").

see also: DIDOT

Coated Paper

A smooth paper finished with a coating of china clay.

Collating

The bringing together of gathered sections in the correct order.

see also: GATHER

Colour

(1) The overall greyness of a page of type when viewed at arms length. (2) The light or heavy appearance of a particular typeface.

Column Rule
A vertical rule between columns of type.

Condensed
Describes type in which the width is narrower in proportion to its height than in normal type.

Copyfitting
Literally, trying to make copy fit the layout by editing text, changing fonts, altering character size, and reducing leading.

Crop Marks
Marks inserted manually or automatically to define the actual page size on oversize bromide or film.

Cropping
The elimination of parts of an illustration or text that are not required to be printed. This allows the remaining parts of the image to be enlarged to fill available space.

Cross Head
A heading set in the body of the text. Used to break up long columns and to draw readers' attention.

Cursive
Type resembling handwriting.

D

Descender
The part of the letter that extends below the base line of other letters, as in j, p, q, and y.

Diacritical Mark
A mark indicating the value or pronunciation of a character.

Didot Point
A unit of type measurement in the European system (0.38mm/0.0148″). 12 didot points equal 1 cicero.

Dipthong

Vowel characters joined for reasons of aesthetics or convenience, such as 'æ' or 'œ'
see also: LIGATURE

Discretionary Hyphen

A user inserted hyphenation point that functions only when a word occurs at a line end.

Display Type

Large type, usually more than 14 point, of the sort used in advertising to make messages more prominent.

Drop Cap

A large initial at the beginning of a paragraph that drops into the lines of type below.
see also: INITIAL

Dummy

A scaled page layout, preliminary drawing, or other representation of a planned publication.

E

Ellipses

The three full points used to indicate that text matter is incomplete, omitted, or to be continued.

Em

A unit of measurement used to define horizontal space. It has no size until a point size has been selected because its size is that of a square whose height and width are the same as that of the typesize in use. Thus a 9 point em will be 9 points high and 9 points wide.

Em Rule/Dash

A dash used in punctuating text the width of one em, i.e. the width of the typesize in points.

En

A space unit one-half the width of an em. Also known as a 'nut'.

En Rule/Dash

A dash half the width of an em.

End Paper

The leaves at the end of a book that join the body to the cover.

Expanded Type

Describes type which is wider in proportion to its height than normal.

F

Face

Refers to a typeface design.

Film

Transparent plastic material coated with photosensitive material for recording a photographic image of type and/or illustration.

Flush

A paragraph margin that is even or not indented. Commonly expressed as flush-left or flush-right, in which the type aligns vertically at the left and right margins respectively.

Folio

The page number. Also a sheet of copy.

Font (also Fount)

The complete assemblage of all characters in a particular style and size of type.

Font Metric

The width and height of each character.

Full Measure

A line of text set to the entire line width.

Full Point

Typographic term for a 'full stop'.

G

Galley
Nowadays, typeset or imageset bromide
returned for proof-reading.

Gather
Collecting pages and sections together.

Grid
A guide used by designers to ensure accurate
and consistent placement of design elements
(text, illustration, etc.) on a layout.

Gothic (also Blackletter)
Old style typeface with no serif and broad even
strokes: based on broad-nib calligraphy.

Grotesque
Another name for sans serif type style.

Gutter
The inside margin of a book where facing pages
join. Also, the white space between adjacent
columns of type.

H

H & J, H/J
Hyphenation and justification.
see also: HYPHENATION

Hairline
The thinnest rule. In desktop publishing, rules
thinner than 0.5 point rarely reproduce well on
300 dpi laser printers.

Hanging Indent
Paragraphs with the first line set flush-left and
the remainder indented.

Hanging Punctuation
Punctuation allowed to fall outside the measure
of a piece of text.

Hard Hyphen

A hyphen created with the hyphen key only and shown whether it falls in the middle or at the end of a line.

see also: DISCRETIONARY HYPHEN

Hyphenation

The use of a hyphen to divide one word between syllables so that it can be broken across a line.

I

Imagesetter

A device for producing combined text and graphical output at high resolution on bromide or film, as distinct from a typesetter which only sets type. Most imagesetters require PostScript files for input.

Imposition

The arrangement of a number of pages being printed on the same sheet so that when the sheet is folded and cut the pages occur in the correct order.

Imprint

Information required by law for all publications. Includes the name and address of the publisher and printer.

Indention

Blank space of fixed width at the beginning of a line of type. Usually employed to denote the beginning of a new paragraph. The amount of indent should be proportional to the line width.

Inferior Characters

Also known as subscript. They are smaller than the body and have a baseline that aligns with the bottom of descenders.

Initial

The first letter of a paragraph that can be modified for a more pleasing visual effect. Dropped caps and raised caps are two forms of modified initial.

Italic

Type that is slanted a fixed amount to the right. Also known as cursive.

J

Justification

The process of adding additional word spacing, letterspacing, and usually hyphenation so that type exactly fills a line (flush left and right).

K

Kerning

A form of negative letterspacing in which space between selected characters is reduced. Also, PAIR KERNING, in which spacing is reduced between standard character pairs, such as AV. Kerning is used to give overall aesthetic appeal to type. Display type in particular requires kerning to reduce excessive white space between characters.

see also: LETTERSPACING

L

Layout

The harmonious assembly of all design elements — type, illustration, etc. — to produce complete pages.

Leaders

Rows of dots or dashes used to guide the eye from one item to another. Particularly used in tables. They should align vertically as well as horizontally.

Leading

("ledding") Spacing between lines and paragraphs measured (generally) from baseline to successive baseline. Usually expressed in points, e.g. 10/12 point would be 10 point type on 12 point leading. Variously known also as line spacing or line separation.

Leaf

The single sheet in a document with a page on each side, e.g. an eight page document contains four leaves.

Letterspacing

Literally the space between letters. Also refers to the process of adding or removing space to aid justification. Also used in display type to produce interesting visual effects.

see also: KERNING, TRACKING

Ligature

Two or more letters brought together to form one character.

Literal

Also known as a 'lit' in the trade. A type error where one character is substituted for another. Also includes transpositions, wrong fonts, and wrong cases.

Loose Lines

Usually found in justified text and caused by excessive word and letterspacing. Hyphenation and reduced spacing alleviates the problem.

Lower Case

Characters in the lower case alphabet, as in a, b, c, etc.

M

Measure

The length of a line of type. Usually measured in picas.

see also: PICAS

Monospaced

A characteristic of a font where all characters occupy the same width. Courier is an example of a monospaced font.

see also: PROPORTIONAL

O

Oblique

A characteristic of a typeface having upright strokes at an angle from the vertical axis. Unlike true italic faces that are individually designed, oblique faces are algorithmically generated from the roman equivalent.

Orphan

A widow carried over to the beginning of the following page. Considered poor typography.

see also: WIDOW

Over Matter

Copy that is too long to fit the designated text area.

P

Page Proofs

The stage following galleyed proofs in which pages are made up and paginated.

Pair Kerning

The adjustment of space between two adjacent characters to improve visual appeal.

Paragraph

A unit of English composition. Should be denoted by a first line indent or additional leading above the first line.

PI Characters

Characters extraneous to the font set such as the amenity and recreation symbols used in tourist guides. Also mathematical or monetary symbols.

Pica

A unit of type measurement. 12 picas equal 1 point.

see also: POINT

PMT

Photo Mechanical Transfer

Point

A unit of type measurement (0.01383″) used in the British-American system (i.e. non-metric). There are approx. 72 points in an inch. 12 points equal 1 pica.

Point Size

The height of the area into which a character is designed to fit, measured in points.

Prelims

Preliminary pages of a document before the main text pages.

Proof

A print of a typeset job examined and read to detect errors.

Proportional Spacing

The set width of individual characters varies in modern typography depending on the width of the character itself. Thus, spacing is proportional to the character width.

Q

Quadding

Inserting blank spaces to fill out a line to a pre-set measure.

R

Ragged

Edges of text not justified in a common alignment.

Recto

The right-hand page of a book.

Register

The accurate positioning of each printing as used in four-colour work. Ensures that successive printing is spot-on each time for crisp results.

Reproduction

The conversion of camera-ready copy and base artwork into lithographic plates for printing.

Reverse

Copy that has white lettering on a black or coloured background.

Rivers

Unattractive connecting areas of white space caused by excessive word spacing or the adjacency of word spaces in justified type. Holding a proof at arms length is a good way to spot rivers.

Roman

Upright type. Also a style of serif type with varying thickness of line.

Run-Around

Arrangement of type around an illustration or box.

Running Head

A title repeated at the top of each page.

S

Sans Serif

Type having no serifs.

Screening

The process of converting continuous tone illustrations into a series of dots or lines for printing.

Serif

A short finishing stroke at the ends of character strokes.

Set

The designed width of a character plus surrounding space.

Small Caps

Small upper case letters usually the same height as a lower case letter of the face in use. Used to give emphasis to a word or phrase in continuous text, or for decorations and titles after a person's name.

Solid (set)

Type in which no additional leading is used between lines other than that built into the type design.

Superior Characters

Also known as superscript. Small letters, figures, or symbols that align with or near the top of capital letters.

T

Thin Space

A space usually one-third or one-quarter of an em space. Always equal to the width of the full-point or comma.

Tracking

Defines degree of universal letterspacing, positve or negative, between characters. Used to specify type requirements, as in tight, normal, open, etc.

see also: LETTERSPACING

Type Family

The complete series of a particular typeface including lightface, boldface, condensed, italic, etc.

Type Styles

General Classification:

(1) **Roman:** commonly used in all kinds of printed matter. An upright type with or without serifs. (2) **Italic:** sloping letters of any face. Used for quotations or emphasis. (3) **Script:** a type face with joined letters imitative of hand writing. (4) **Sans serif:** type with lines of uniform thickness and without serifs. (5) **Titling:** a design with no lower case in which caps fill the whole depth of the type body.

Typography

The general term for the art of type composition, letter assembly, and design.

U

Unit System

Measurement system employed in typesetting to subdivide units of horizontal space. Thus the 18 unit system divides an em into 18 equal vertical slices. Like the em, units are proportional to point size. 54 or 72 unit systems are also employed for very fine work.

Upper Case

Capital letters.

V

Verso

The left-hand page of a book.

W

Waist Line

Line above the baseline defining the top of the x-height.

Weight

The degree of boldness of typeface. The various subdivisions, light, bold, extra-bold, etc. are not standard across typefaces.

White Space

That part of printed matter not covered by text or illustration.

Widow

A single word or phrase covering less than one-third of the line width at the end of a paragraph. To be avoided if possible.

X

x-height

The height of lower case letters without ascenders or descenders, such as 'x'.

Typography & DTP

Today's desktop publishing software gives you the tools to produce documents to very high typographical standards. To do this, however, unless you are already well versed in the art, you must invest some time in study. And, even if you are well versed, you will still need to invest some time in exploring the darker recesses of your software so that you can put into practice what you already know.

Obviously good typography doesn't happen by accident. You must have a clear idea at the outset of what you are trying to achieve. If you aren't a designer find someone who is and use your software to implement their design. Even so, having a good overall design does not guarantee good typography. That's what this book is about: the detail of putting type on the page so that it is most appealing to the reader.

These days, when I pick up a brochure or a book I look at it to see if I can tell whether it has been desktop published. With good ones it can be impossible to tell, with others there are tell-tale signs that point to an obviously desktop published document, produced by someone with little understanding of typography. The main ones are listed below, look out for them in documents that you receive over the desk and avoid them in yours.

Beware of Default Options

Software developers try to be kind to their users and build default choices into their products. These may be OK for the 'average' document but they are far from OK once you start getting creative.

To develop and maintain a professional look you have to go beyond the choices that are made for you and start making a few of your own. These choices must be informed. You must know what you are trying to achieve typographically, and you must know how to make the software do it for you. This book will, I hope, 'bust' some of the jargon that you will find in your software manuals and make you a little less intimidated by the terminology that you find there.

Key Combinations

Get to know the extended ASCII character set. Many of the tell-tale signs listed below are overcome by using characters that you won't find keys for on the keyboard. They are all there, you just need to know what to press with what.

Your software manual will tell you which keys to press to produce em dashes and proper opening and closing double quotes. It will also tell you how to get discretionary hyphens, thin spaces, figure spaces, and how to kern words and characters. Yes, sometimes you do have to read the manual, but the manual won't tell you what to read. By using this book you should be able to go straight to the index of your manual to find what you need to know.

Obviously DTP

Below is a list of tell-tale signs that point to an obviously desktop published document.

Hyphenated headlines
Hyphenation should always be turned off for headlines and captions.

Dashes
Find the keys to produce the longer em dash ('—') and the en dash ('-') on your keyboard. Use them in place of the hyphen ('-') where appropriate.

Bad justification
Don't use justified type on narrow line widths. Use hyphenation to avoid loose lines. Don't have more than two successive hyphens.

Italics
Should be used sparingly and only for things like emphasis (even then bold is actually better), names of plays, foreign words (see A–Z section for full list). While they may look attractive they reduce legibility in long text passages.

Typefaces and fonts
Use only one or two per document. If you want variety then use different weights or styles of the same typeface.

Letterspacing in captions
Tighten it up! This is definitely one where the software defaults won't do.

Indents
Don't use indents AND additional leading to signify new paragraphs. It's either/or. Don't indent the first paragraph at the start of a page or after a heading unless you are using an indented raised initial.

Small Caps
Use small caps rather than normal caps for emphasis in text. They are still obvious but they don't disrupt the line height.

Auto leading
Set your own! Different typefaces and typestyles have their own requirements (see table in A–Z section). Also, try and keep to a consistent leading value or a multiple of the body text leading throughout your document.

Tint boxes
Use them sparingly and reserve them for headings or for small text panels. Keep the tints light so that the text can still be read.

Rules and boxes
Leave enough room above and below rules to give the type space to 'breathe'. If you box text then leave enough space to the

left and right, and above and below so that the type doesn't look squashed in the box.

Column alignment

Columns don't have to align vertically at the bottom of the page but the lines should align horizontally. Some software (e.g. Ventura) will help you do this automatically, with others you will need to do it by hand.

Underlining

If you are using it for emphasis save it for the typewriter. Use something else like emboldening or small caps.

All caps and reverses

Don't set long passages of text all in upper case as it markedly reduces legibility. Upper case letters have a consistent outline whereas our eye has been trained over many years to recognise letters and words by the differences in their outline. Also, don't set long passages as white out of black as this too reduces legibility.

Punctuation

A subject on its own but a few points to note are as follows.

quotation marks: double and single quotes should appear as " " and ' ' respectively. If (as I recommend you do for longer documents) you create and maintain text in a word processor a number of things can happen to quotation marks when you load the text into your DTP software depending on the combination of software you use.

The opening single quote invariably ends up the same as the closing one or they both are represented as 'foot' marks (i.e. the old notation for pre-decimal linear measurement). Similarly, double quotes either end up both the same or as two 'inch' marks.

This problem can be overcome in a number of ways. The first and easiest is to use DTP software that does the conversion for you. Alternatively, you can insert the ASCII codes in you word processor files, or you can edit the text in your DTP software.

lists: the use of ':-' preceding a vertical list is outmoded: just the colon will do. Also, on a point of style, the paragraph before a list should always contain a phrase such as 'the following:' or 'as follows:'. This has the effect of leading (rather than dropping) the reader into a list.

semi-colon: the semi-colon is probably the most abused punctuation mark in the English language. Don't use it to separate items in a paragraph list. The basic rule is that you can replace a semi-colon with a full-stop without destroying the sense. What follows a semi-colon should be a sentence, i.e. complete with a verb. If you don't know how to use a semi-colon, don't until you understand how.

Copy

Just as poor typography provides tell-tale signs so does poorly written copy. DTP provides an overwhelming temptation to

---

do it all yourself: including copywriting. Unfortunately, an English 'O' level doesn't make you a copywriter. Badly written copy shows you up every time, no matter how good your design is. Be critical of your own writing and actively seek constructive criticism from other people.

25 Top Tips

You will find below 25 tips that cover some of the most important things to look out for when designing a type layout. Many of the points are expanded further in the A–Z section of this book.

1. Remember — good design is as much experimentation as inspiration.

2. If your caption goes over two lines break it by sense.

3. Use no more than two successive hyphens.

4. Use a condensed typeface to fit copy into small areas.

5. Distinguish between hyphens and dashes. Learn to use them correctly.

6. Experiment with drop caps and other sorts of paragraph lead-ins.

7. Don't use italics or reversed text for long text passages.

8. Don't use justified alignment on long lines, especially with sans serif type.

9. Adjust letterspacing to give the most readable configuration. Be sure to reduce letterspacing on large headlines.

10. Parentheses in desktop publishing are designed to centre on lower case letters. They should be raised when used with caps. The same applies to dashes which are also centred on lower case letters.

11. Use the correct line width for the type size in use (see table in A–Z section).

12. Signal new paragraphs either by additional leading or indention (not both).

13. Use serif type on long text passages. It is less tiring to the eye and quicker to read.

14. Use small caps for emphasis in body text. They are less disruptive to line height.

15. Distiguish between the x-height and overall height of type. x-height may be a better criteria for choosing a face for a particular purpose.

16. When using very small type, choose a face with a large x-height.

17. Keep word spacing and letterspacing tight.

18. Experiment with different weights of the same typeface.

19. Use only a few typefaces, i.e. 1 or 2, when designing your layout.

20. White space invites the reader in and adds flexibility to your layouts.

21. Always use captions with photographs or illustrations. They are read more than body copy.

22. A short first paragraph aids legibility.

23. If you can't find a typeface that suits your message, simply use a legible one.

24. The best time to edit copy is before you send files for imagesetting.

25. If your final product is laser-printed output consider using coloured paper to add variety to an otherwise black & white product.

A–Z Section

Caption

Also known as headlines, captions are the headings used at the top of pages or columns of type, or the large display letters used for advertisements. 14 to 30 point type is generally used.

There is no one typeface that should be used as every printed message has its own appropriate face. Choose one that the reflects the mood or content of your subject matter.

Experiment with the following styles for captions:

- ALL CAPS
- only IMPORTant letters in caps
- all first letters of Main Words in caps
- all lowercase
- most **important words** bolder
- most important words different style
- most IMPORTANT WORDS all caps
- most *imporant words* all italics
- most important words in colour

Picture Captions

Captions, in another sense, are also used to provide explanatory labels for pictures or illustrations. All pictures should have a caption because people read them more than body copy (look at *National Geographic*). Try to keep them to about 10 words in length.

How should you set picture captions? Avoid using italics. Try instead using the body face 1 point smaller, or the body face 2 points larger. Either of these options can also be bolded if required. Another variant is to use your display face at body size.

**There's Only One Way from
Karachi to Kathmandhu**

**There's Only One Way
from Karachi to Kathmandhu**

above: if your caption runs to two lines (it should
never be more than two lines) be sure to break the
lines by sense rather than just fit. In the second
(correct) example above each line is a complete clause.

Colour

see also: hyphenation, letterspacing, weight

Typographically speaking colour refers to the overall grey tone of a body of text. The best way of observing this is to hold a page proof at arms length. You can try turning it upside down as well. This has the effect of preventing you from trying to read the page rather than looking at its overall structure.

The required even tone can be disrupted by bad word breaks, bad character spacing, uneven leading, or excessive hyphenation. Justified text is particularly prone to RIVERS — connecting areas of white space caused by too much word spacing. They can be eliminated by adjusting word spacing or letterspacing, or by economical use of hyphenation.

Check the following:

- keep word and letterspacing consistent
- keep widows and orphans to a minimum
- kern poorly spaced words and phrases
- no more than 2 successive hyphens

The term colour is also used to refer to the WEIGHT of type. That is the lightness or darkness of a particular typeface when printed.

Condensed & Expanded

CONDENSED describes the relative narrowness of all characters in a typeface, i.e. the alphabet occupies less width. Condensed typefaces are useful when it is necessary to fit copy into a space that won't accommodate a normal face.

EXPANDED describes a variation in type width where characters are wider than in the normal alphabet. Its use is usually restricted to headlines, subheads, and small blocks of advertising copy. It is not as legible as standard type and should not be used with short line widths.

Typography
Typography
Typography

above: condensed, normal, and expanded versions of the same typeface. All are 18 point type. Note in particular the wide variation in width occupied by the different styles.

Dashes

see also: En & Em

There are actually four types of dash used in typography but only two or three are readily available to the desktop publisher. They lend subtlety to your documents and you should learn when and how to use them. They are as follows:

hyphen: used for breaking words on syllables at the end of lines to provide even spacing in justified text. Also used in connected words, e.g. 'day-to-day'.

en dash: used as shorthand for the word to (or through), as in 'items 3–6'. Also used to connect nouns of equal weight, as in 'north–south divide'. It is the en dash too that can act as a colon. The en dash should always appear with no space on either side ('closed'), i.e. not 3 – 6 but 3–6.

em dash: used to indicate missing text or for parenthetical remarks to show an aside or to provide special emphasis. For example:

The plane flew — but only just — clawing its way into the clear tropical sky.

Like the en dash, the em dash can also be used to replace a colon. It can be either open or closed. Used open it provides more alternatives for line breaks.

3/4 em dash: just a small em dash. Used where the em dash looks too wide for the typeface in use. This dash is not generally available in desktop publishing packages.

Dashes should not be carried over to the beginning of a following line. Also, when using a condensed typeface, a narrow en dash is better than a full em dash.

Ellipses

see also: En & Em

The three (and only three) full points
indicating something is missing or that the
flow of dialogue or narrative has been
interrupted.

If they follow a complete sentence
the full point is also included, i.e. four
successive full points. The spacing
between the ellipses should be the same in
each case. This means that you should use
fixed width spaces to separate them rather
than normal word spaces. For example:

*The arctic weather was at its most violent, and
they had experienced fierce storms the night
before. The tents were buried under fresh snow.*

becomes

*. . . they had experienced fierce storms the
night before. The tents were buried under fresh
snow.*

or

*The arctic weather was at its most violent, and
they had experienced fierce storms the night
before. . . .*

Emphasis

see also: initials, small caps

Desktop publishing provides for many varieties of emphasis. They should all be used economically. Most people resort to setting text in italics when adding emphasis but emboldening is actually more effective. Underlining should be avoided and is really a redundant hangover from typewriter days.

To emphasise words or phrases in text try one of the following:

- boldface
- italic
- size (smaller or larger)
- devices (e.g. bullets)
- colour
- caps
- different style

First lines are important for getting the reader 'in'. There are a number of effects that you can employ to add emphasis to first lines. Try some of these:

- indent
- outdent
- raised cap
- drop cap
- a device such as a symbol or logo
- run the first 2 to 3 words as small caps

- opening small sentence in italics
- opening phrase in boldface
- ellipses
- extra space before and after a paragraph

Heaving seas rolled against the sides of the polar-bound ice breaker *Endymion.* Two days previously they had received a distress call from the exploration party stranded on an ice floe.

above: an indented raised initial used as a paragraph lead-in. Research shows that such devices are very good for getting the reader 'in' to documents.

En & Em

The en and em are fixed width units used in type measurement. An en is one-half an em, and neither has any value until a point size is selected.

The em unit is a square whose height and width are the same as the point size. Thus a 9 point em is nine points high and nine points wide. The size of an em is therefore variable and directly proportional to the point size in use. The en is the same height as the em but is only half the width.

En and em spaces are used to specify fixed-width blank spaces since, in typography, word spaces vary in width. That's why you can't use word spaces (entered with the spacebar) for indents. The width of the space will vary depending on line width. Instead, indents are specified in ems (or picas).

There are two other types of fixed-width space: the FIGURE SPACE and the THIN SPACE. Sometimes the en space is used as the figure space. A thin space is either one-quarter or one-third of an em.

Note that the em space is not equal to the width of a capital 'M' as many people believe. This may be a convenient rule of thumb in some cases, but actually bares no resemblance to the actual definition of the em.

Ems are also used to specify limits of word and letterspacing.

Gutter

see also: justified, ragged

The empty space separating columns of type. The actual width of gutter used depends very much on the page design and the number of columns in use.

In general, gutter space should be at least one pica, especially for justified type. Gutter space can be slightly less for ragged type as no line extends the full column width.

Column rules

If it is necessary to use very narrow gutters vertical rules can be used to prevent columns running together. Vertical rules are nearly always a good idea when ragged type is used in columns.

If justified type is used, however, the use of vertical rules often looks overdone since the even alignment of justified columns forms an optical column boundary in its own right.

Heaving seas rolled against the sides of the polar-bound ice breaker *Endymion*. Two days previously they had received a distress call from the exploration party stranded on an ice floe. They were only 30 nautical miles from the position reported by radio during the last contact: but the going was tough. The temperature was falling rapidly with the onset of the arctic winter, and the rate of ice formation had increased alarmingly.

Heaving seas rolled against the sides of the polar-bound ice breaker *Endymion*. Two days previously they had received a distress call from the exploration party stranded on an ice floe. They were only 30 nautical miles from the position reported by radio during the last contact: but the going was tough. The temperature was falling rapidly with the onset of the arctic winter, and the rate of ice formation had increased alarmingly.

above: the first example shows ragged type used with column rules to define column boundaries. In the second example the text is justified and set without rules; the even vertical alignment defining the column boundaries.

Hyphenation

see also: justified, ragged

The process of manually or automatically breaking words into syllables and inserting hyphens. Hyphenation is used so that word spaces remain consistent for proper justification. The following guidelines should be observed:

- there must be at least two characters either side of the hyphen
- avoid hyphenating headlines
- don't hyphenate single syllable words
- don't hyphenate on a double consonant (e.g. poss-ible not pos-sible) unless the word ends in a double consonant
- don't use more than two hyphens in a row unless you have to

Hyphenation should be kept to a minimum for maximum legibility. It is best used on justified text to prevent loose lines, i.e. those with excessive word spacing. If you must hyphenate, never have more than two (some authorities say three) successive hyphens.

Most desktop publishing packages come with hyphenation dictionaries built in and provide for automatic or manual (prompted) hyphenation. You will also encounter the discretionary hyphen.

Discretionary Hyphenation

If you manually enter a hyphen from the keyboard you create a hard hyphen. If you re-lay text and a word containing a hard hyphen is placed in the middle of a line the hyphen will still show. To overcome this desktop publishing packages provide facilities for inserting discretionary hyphens that will only cause a word to be hyphenated if it occurs at the end of a line.

Like many special effects in DTP software, discretionary hyphens are created by a special combination of keystrokes (e.g. 'CONTROL' + '-' in Ventura).

Indention

Indention is the addition of space before lines of text so that they are offset from the left and/or right margins. Indention may be applied to all or selected lines in a paragraph. Indention is the same thing as indentation but indention is actually the correct term.

Indents are a useful means of indicating the start of new paragraphs. Additional leading between paragraphs has the same effect. Research has shown that indention actually increases reading speed. If you choose indention to identify new paragraphs you should use at least an em of indent.

The first paragraph following a heading should not be indented (unless you are using an initial) and the amount of indent should be proportional to the line length as follows:

under 24 picas — 1 em space
25-36 picas — 1.5 em spaces
37 picas or more — 2 em spaces

There are many forms of paragraph indent. One commonly used and referred to is the HANGING INDENT in which the first line goes across the full measure and all remaining lines in the paragraph are indented.

Heaving seas rolled against the
sides of the polar-bound ice breaker
Endymion. Two days previously they had
received a distress call from the
exploration party stranded on an ice floe.

Heaving seas rolled against the sides of the
polar-bound ice breaker *Endymion.* Two
days previously they had received a
distress call from the exploration party
stranded on an ice floe.

above: two types of paragraph indent. The first is a
first line indent used to indicate the start of a new
paragraph and the second is a hanging indent in which
lines of text 'hang' from an outdented first line.

Initials

see also: emphasis

Initials are emphasised letters at the start of a paragraph, usually the first one of a chapter. The most commonly encountered initial is the drop cap where the first letter of a paragraph drops into the body of the text occupying multiple lines. The raised cap is also used where the initial sits several lines above the body but rests on the same baseline as the first line of the paragraph.

Research shows that drop and raised caps are very effective at getting readers into a document. They are also useful for breaking up long text passages.

An initial must always align at the base of a line of text. Optical alignment can be improved by slightly outdenting the cap from the body. The space at the side of the initial should be optically the same as that below. Setting the first word following the initial in caps provides a pleasing effect. A further variation is to indent a raised initial.

H eaving seas rolled against the sides of the polar bound ice-breaker *Endymion*. Two days previously they had received a distress call from the exploration party stranded on an ice floe.

H eaving seas rolled against the sides of the polar bound ice-breaker *Endymion*. Two days previously they had received a distress call from the exploration party stranded on an ice floe.

H eaving seas rolled against the sides of the polar bound ice-breaker *Endymion*. Two days previously they had received a distress call from the exploration party stranded on an ice floe.

above: variations on the theme of initials. First a dropped initial (or 'drop cap'), second a raised initial, and third an indented raised initial.

Italic

A characteristic of a typeface that has upright strokes at an angle to the vertical axis. Italics were first used in the sixteenth century and were designed so that publishers could produce smaller books.

True italics are designed separately unlike so-called machine italics which are generated algorithmically by slanting the roman equivalent of the same typeface. The terms italic, cursive and oblique are nowadays almost synonymous.

Italics should be used sparingly as they can be overly decorative and difficult to read. New users of desktop publishing are prone to using some of the highly decorative faces that are available because they look 'nice'. Maybe they do, but they are difficult to read on long passages of text and should certainly not be used for business letters.

The following can reasonably be set in italic: titles of publications, names of ships, trains and aircraft, foreign words and phrases, scientific names, quotations, names of shows, plays and works of art.

Italic type is often used for emphasising words or phrases in body type but is actually less effective·than bolding.

Reviewing the newly published *Polar Conquests*, Price commented that . . .

In his letter to *The Sunday Times*, Major Uprising wrote . . .

At the opening night of *In a Nutshell*, the most outstanding performance was by . . .

Although lacking in certain areas the book was a useful *aide mémoire* said . . .

The Common Foxglove, *digitalis purpurea*, is just one of many plants . . .

above: examples of some uses of italic type in text.

Justification

see also: colour, ragged

The even alignment of text at both the left and the right margins. It is achieved by filling a line until the last word or syllable fits, and then dividing the remaining space by the number of word spaces. The result is then placed at each word space to give variable word spacing from line to line.

For long text passages ragged right text is better because the eye needs to return to a reference line on the left. Justified text usually requires hyphenation to avoid loose lines and rivers that mar the typographical colour of a page. Recent research finds that justification makes little difference to overall legibility but may reduce reading speed.

Vertical Justification

Text can also be justified between top and bottom margins so that text always fills columns exactly or so that the column bottoms are always at the same level.

The first effect is achieved by FEATHERING where the exact amount of space required to make text fill a column is added by increasing space between paragraphs. The second is CARDING where space is added in multiples of body text leading. This ensures that lines of text always align horizontally although the text may not exactly reach the page bottom.

Heaving seas rolled against the sides of the polar-bound ice breaker *Endymion*. Two days previously they had received a distress call from the exploration party stranded on an ice floe. They were only 30 nautical miles from the position reported by radio during the last contact: but the going was tough. The temperature was falling rapidly with the onset of the arctic winter, and the rate of ice formation had increased alarmingly.

above: justified text aligns vertically at both the left and right margins. Hyphenation is often required to avoid the development of unsightly 'rivers'.

Leaders

see also: en & em

As the name implies, a string of dots or dashes that 'lead' the eye from one line to another. The effect is often used in a table of contents or a price list. Note that leader characters must align vertically as well as horizontally.

It may be better from a reader's perspective not to use leaders in a table of contents at all. Just run the page number right after the chapter heading set of by an em space. This often makes the contents page easier to use, even though it doesn't look as neat.

Try as an alternative putting the page number before the title, or even using a hairline rule extending the full width under both title and page number.

above: using leaders (top) may not be best for the reader when laying out a table of contents. Try instead (middle) putting page numbers right after chapter or section names or (bottom) running a hairline rule underneath the text and the numbers.

Leading

see also: type size

Today, leading (or line spacing) is generally defined as the distance from a baseline to the baseline of the line below (or above). The baseline being the horizontal point at which a line of type rests.

Sans serif type should always have ample leading and should never be set solid (i.e. when the leading value is the same as the point size, also termed zero-leading). Bold type requires more leading than normal type. In general, heavier type faces need more leading than light ones. All faces are more legible with a moderate amount of leading.

Leading should be about 20% of the point size. Use the table on the next page as a guide. Maximum values are best used for sans serif type.

Type Size	Minimum Leading	Optimum Leading	Maximum Leading
6	6	7	7
7	7	8	8.5
8	8	9.5	10
9	9	11	12
10	10	12	13
11	12	13	14
12	14	15	16

above: table of leading values for various point sizes. In keeping with current practice, leading is specified as distance from baseline to baseline of successive lines.

Legibility

see also: leading, type size, x-height

Legibility, the ease with which a passage of text can be read, is the result of effective typography. Any page layout should have overall aesthetic appeal and should hold a reader's attention. Obviously the actual copy must interest the reader but even the best copy will be to no avail if the reader is immediately put off by poor typography.

Recent research indicates that narrower line widths, consistent word spacing, and well-designed typefaces all aid efficient reading. Reverse type, type in all caps, and bold or light versions of a particular typeface all detract from legibility.

These factors are more than just scientific observations. The easier someone finds text to read, the greater their interest and retention will be. This is as important in an advert as in a novel. Remember: what is most legible is also most appealing to the reader.

Other findings show that serif typefaces with a large x-height are the most legible. Also word spacing should be the width of a lowercase 'i' of the typeface in use, and leading should always be slightly larger than word spacing.

Letterspacing

see also: word spacing

This general term embraces several other typographical functions such as kerning and tracking. All are explained below.

LETTERSPACING is the space between letters. It can be both positive and negative. In positive letterspacing space is added between letters, usually for aesthetic reasons in all cap headlines or logotypes. Its use is not generally recommended because it reduces legibility and interrupts the even texture usually required of type. Negative spacing is where space is subtracted equally between all letters. This may also be necessary for aesthetic reasons.

Unless you are striving for a specific effect, be sure to reduce letterspacing in large captions when using DTP software. Too much letterspacing in large fonts is one of the tell-tale signs of an obviously desktop-published document. Generally, DTP software uses default letterspacing settings which are optimal for body size type. If you don't reduce spacing as the typesize increases you will find unsightly gaps appearing. It is difficult to say what the right amount is since it varies from typesize to typesize, and from typeface to typeface. You will need to experiment to find the optimal settings for the typefaces you use.

When specifying type it is possible to request a degree of TRACKING, such as tight or open, which is simply a preset amount of universal negative letterspacing. This may be done to achieve a particular colour of type.

Selective reduction in letterspacing is called KERNING and is usually applied to specific character pairs. It is usually display size typefaces that require kerning to provide an overall pleasing optical effect.

Most quality desktop publishing packages provide facilities for automatic pair kerning, and for interactively kerning or letterspacing words and character pairs.

Heaving seas rolled against the sides of the polar-bound ice breaker *Endymion*. Two days previously they had received a distress call from the exploration party stranded on an ice floe.

They were only 30 nautical miles from the position reported by radio during the last contact: but the going was tough. The temperature was falling rapidly with the onset of the arctic winter, and the rate of ice formation had increased alarmingly.

above: letterspacing can be either positive or negative. Too much (top) has the effect of breaking up individual words and reducing readability. Too little (bottom) produces an equally undesirable 'cramped' look. Note also the effect on the perceived size and colour of the type. Both examples are the same size.

Line width

see also: leading, point system, type size

Literally the distance between margins, or column boundaries, also referred to as measure or set width. The right line width to use depends on type size, leading and, to a lesser extent, the type face in use.

For type sizes in the range 9-12 point, 10-12 words per line is easiest on the eye. This equates to a line width of 18-24 picas. For type in the range 7-8 point, a line width of 12 picas is most legible. Double columns of maximum line width are more readable than single columns with long lines. For instance, 2 columns of 17 picas is more readable than 1 column of 32 picas width.

In general, reading is less efficient with lines that are too long or too short. Small type on short lines makes for lively and flexible layouts, long lines are better for prolonged reading. Short lines and long lines of sans serif type are best set ragged.

The most legible line width is also the most aesthetically pleasing. The formulae below and the table on the next page provide useful guidelines on suitable line widths for various type sizes.

1. Point size of type x 2 = line length in picas

2. Length of line = width of lc* alphabet x 1.5
    *lower case

Type Size	Minimum Length	Optimum Length	Maximum Length
6	8	10	12
7	8	11	14
8	9	13	16
9	10	14	18
10	13	16	20
11	13	18	22
12	14	21	24

above: table showing acceptable line widths for various type sizes. (Type sizes are in points, line widths in picas.)

Numbers

Old style numerals with differentiating ascenders and descenders are more legible than Modern Roman. Generally, diagrams are superior to tables when it comes to reader retention, but tables are actually preferred by readers.

Grouping numerals in vertical groups of 5 aids location of items in a table. Also, approximately 1 pica of space or 1 pica space with a rule is equally effective in separating columns. Tabular matter should be at least 8 point with generous leading. Items in the first column should be bolded. Tints can also be used for additional emphasis (see example next page).

	48	50	53	54
12	**108.0**	112.5	119.3	121.5
13	**99.7**	103.8	110.0	112.2
14	**92.5**	96.4	102.2	104.0
15	**86.4**	90.0	95.4	97.2
16	**81.0**	84.4	89.4	91.1
17	**76.2**	79.4	84.2	85.8
18	**72.0**	75.0	79.5	81.0
19	**68.0**	71.0	75.3	76.7
20	**64.8**	67.5	71.6	73.0
21	**62.0**	64.3	68.1	69.4

above: grouping numerals in vertical groups of 5 aids location of items in a table. Other refinements include the use of tint panels and emboldening of items in the first column.

Fxtgd

above: the relationship of point size to type 'height'. The example above is 72 point type. The outermost lines are 72 points apart. As you can see, neither the cap-height nor the height from ascender to descender is 72 points. This underlines the fact that the point size for all typefaces includes a built-in amount of leading.

Point size

see also: type size, x–height

A strict but seemingly vague definition of how point size is measured would say, 'the height of the area into which a character is designed to fit measured in points'.

The definition is important because the measurement of type comes from the days of hot-metal typesetting when it was the size of the metal block that carried the type — the body — which determined the point size, and not the height of the impression made by the type. A brief digression into history is instructive here.

Many of the typefaces in use today were designed or re-designed for hot-metal typesetting. To produce physically separate lines of type it was necessary to add a small amount of leading above and below a character. This might mean that although the impression made by the type was 8 points in height, it was carried on a body that was, say, 10 points in height and would be termed 10 point even though the impression was physically smaller.

Today, most type foundries producing type for desktop publishers have reverted to hot-metal designs where the design provides for a small amount of leading above and below characters. What this means is that measuring the cap-height of a typeface is not a true indication of point size. Some condensed or light faces, for example, are the result of reducing character size on a fixed body height. The impression of a 9 point condensed face might actually be only 7 points high, but would still be termed 9 point in terms of the size of the body on which it sits.

If you don't know the size of a typeface the easiest way to measure it is to get a sample that is set solid, i.e. zero-leaded, and then measure the height from one baseline to the next.

Some authorities suggest that type size is the height from top of ascender to bottom of descender. This serves only to confuse things further. This may be a useful means of comparing typefaces but since this does not include the size of the body it does not provide a figure for the point size of the type.

Fortunately, typesizes are specified for us in desktop publishing packages, and we do not have to be overly concerned with their measurement. And even if we do have to match an existing sample, it is a simple matter to produce output of various sizes that can be cross-matched with the original.

Point system

Typography has its own units of measurement — the point system. There are 2 systems used in Europe at present, the English/American system using points and picas, and the European system using the didot point and the cicero.

Attempts to regularise the measurement of type go back to 1737, the time of Fournier, who was the first to propose a unified system of type measurement and, shortly after in 1785, the Didot family gave their name to the European system of measurement based on the then French inch that is used today. The Anglo-American system was defined in 1886 by the United States Typefounders Association.

ENGLISH/AMERICAN: a point measures 0.01383″, and there are 12 points in a pica, and 6 picas to the inch — but not quite. The relationship is a good *aide mémoire* but 30 picas doesn't exactly equal 5″, but 4.98″.

EUROPEAN: a didot point measures 0.38mm (0.0148″). There are 12 didot points in a cicero (i.e 4.52mm/0.178″).

Although it may seem confusing (and unnecessary) at first, it is worth getting to know the point system since everyone else in the trade uses it too.

Proportional type

Typewriters and line-printers use so-called monospace type where all characters are the same width.

Proportional type, however, comprises characters with differing widths and differing amounts of space allocated to each character depending on character shape and typeface. Thus a letter 'i' is narrower than a letter 'm'. Proportional type is a great aid to legibility since one of the factors that determines character recognition is the surrounding space.

Many users of desktop publishing are tempted, initially, to use the typewriting practice of using spaces to indent text. This will not work with proportionally spaced type since the amount of indent will vary depending on the width of the line. For this reason, fixed width spaces or tabs must be used for indents to avoid uneven vertical alignment.

a i m t w

a i m t w

above: (top) monospaced type in which all characters
are the same width and occupy the same space and
(bottom) proportional type with varying character
widths and variable spacing.

Ragged

see also: justified

Refers to lines of type that are not justified. Designers distinguish between soft ragged in which hyphenation is generally allowed to give a more even line length (but still not justified), and hard ragged where no hyphenation is used and line lengths are more varied.

You will also encounter terms that are equivalent. For example ranged left, flush left and left aligned are the same as ragged right. Similarly, ranged right, flush right and right aligned are the same as ragged left. Flush left and right would be justified.

Heaving seas rolled against the sides of the polar-bound ice breaker *Endymion*. Two days previously they had received a distress call from the exploration party stranded on an ice floe.

Heaving seas rolled against the sides of the polar-bound ice breaker *Endymion*. Two days previously they had received a dis-tress call from the exploration party stranded on an ice floe.

Heaving seas rolled against the sides of the polar-bound ice breaker *Endymion*. Two days previously they had received a distress call from the exploration party stranded on an ice floe.

above: the same paragraph set successively hard-ragged (top), soft-ragged (middle), and justified (bottom).

Serif & sans serif

Serif faces have serifs — lines crossing the free end of a stroke — and sans serif faces don't. The term grotesque is a virtual synonym for sans serif today.

Serif faces comprise the largest group of typefaces and it is generally agreed that serifs were originally a means used by Roman engravers to start a chisel in a new block of stone. Many of the serif typefaces used today date back to the fifteenth and eighteenth centuries. The earliest sans serif typeface was introduced by William Caslon IV in 1816.

Serif faces are marginally more legible than sans serif, and are more frequently used for lengthy text passages because the serifs have the effect of leading the eye and tying letters of a word together. Sans serif faces tend, however, to be better perceived in captions.

There are various types of serif and there are good reasons, usually historical, why so many different types exist. For example, the so-called slab or Egyptian serifed faces (e.g. Rockwell) were introduced following The Industrial Revolution and were influenced, as the name suggests, by the rediscovery of the ancient Egyptian civilisation.

above: examples of serif and, far right, sans serif type.
Note the different types of serif which are, from the
left, bracket (Times), slab (Rockwell),
wedge (Optima). The sans face on the far right is
Helvetica.

Small caps

see also: emphasis, initial

Capital letters that match the x-height of a particular typeface and size. Words appearing in text as all caps are better as small caps because they maintain typographic colour and don't disrupt the height of a line.

Don't mix full and small caps — it looks like a typographic error. The other use for small caps is for titles, awards, decorations, etc., that follow a persons name.

Most desktop publishing software uses *pseudo* small caps which are merely normal caps reduced to the x-height of the current font or some user-specified value. True small caps are designed separately and are scaled down in all proportions. True small caps are becoming available as downloadable font packs for desktop publishers.

HEAVING SEAS rolled against the sides of the polar-bound ice breaker *Endymion*. Two days previously they had received a distress call from the exploration party stranded on an ice floe.

HEAVING SEAS rolled against the sides of the polar-bound ice breaker *Endymion*. Two days previously they had received a distress call from the exploration party stranded on an ice floe.

above: using small caps (bottom) as a paragraph lead-in has a more pleasing effect than normal caps (top) which disrupt the line height.

Type selection

see also: legibility, point size, x-height

When choosing a typeface, ask yourself the following:

- does the type complement the message?
- will the type fit the available space?
- is the typeface available?
- is the copy interesting?
- is the type right for the reader?
- does the type comply with corporate standards?
- will the face encourage people to read?
- is the type contemporary?
- is the face different from that of a competitors?

If you are having difficulty finding a typeface to suit your purpose, simply use one that is legible. Old typesetting hands have a saying, "When in doubt, use Caslon.", which is reckoned to be one of the most legible typefaces ever designed.

The variety of typefaces is bewildering at first, especially when trying to match one used in an existing document. The following 'tell-tale' characters will lead you to the right match on most occasions:

T A g e r t a

Size of Type

When selecting type for body copy your aim should be achieving maximum legibility. For type sizes with a small x-height, 11 or 12 point type should be used. For type with large x-height, 9 or 10 point is best.

Generally speaking, type sizes in the range 9 to 12 point provide maximum legibility. Large type increases the number of reader fixations and causes words to be perceived as sections not whole words. This results in slower reading. Smaller type simply reduces visibility.

If you are producing a publication for reference, a smaller type size than that required for optimal legibility can be used to maximise use of available space. The assumption is that reference material is not for sustained reading. The larger the type used, the lighter its weight can be.

When designing an advert for a magazine that's facing relevant editorial, make the advert typesize bigger than the editorial. Publications for children or older people should use bigger type.

Weight

The lightness or darkness of a particular typeface when printed. Standard gradations are extralight, light, semilight, regular, medium, semibold, bold, extrabold, and heavy (or black). It is important to note that these gradations are not standard across typefaces.

If you use typesetting bureaux you should bear in mind that different weights can be created artificially due to variations in the performance of typesetting equipment. This can be particularly important if you are trying to match accurately a typeface that has been used for a previous job.

The temperature

The temperature

The temperature

The temperature

above: different weights of the same typeface
(Helvetica). From the top: light, normal, bold, and
black.

Widows & orphans

A widow is a short line at the end of a paragraph that is less than one third of the line length. If a widow is carried to the top of the following page it becomes an orphan. Orphans should be avoided altogether, and widows too if possible. Avoid starting a new paragraph as the last line on a page or column.

The temperature was falling rapidly with the onset of the arctic winter, and the rate of ice formation had increased alarmingly. Everyday, the lookout in the crow's nest reported more icebergs. Fog too was becoming a handicap to rapid progress.

above: short lines at the end of a paragraph are termed 'widows'. When carried over to the beginning of a page (below) they are termed 'orphans'. Widows should be avoided if possible; orphans should always be avoided.

progress.

Despite the worsening conditions, the Captain remained confident of reaching the stranded party before their supplies ran out.

Word spacing

see also: colour, letterspacing

Literally the amount of spacing between words. In modern typography word spacing can be varied unlike a typewriter which has spaces of fixed width.

Justification depends on this variability and word spacing is different from line to line. This is one of the reasons why justified text is read more slowly; the eye does not get used to even spacing between words and has to re-adjust on every line.

Word spacing can have a minimum, optimum, or maximum setting. Optimum word spacing should be about the width of a lower case 'i' of the font and size in use. In ragged right type the optimum setting is used throughout. Minimum and maximum spacing comes into play in justified type and is used to prevent loose or tight lines that may adversely affect typographic colour.

Observe the following guidelines wherever possible:

condensed type — less word spacing

small type — more word spacing

expanded type — more word spacing

large type — more word spacing

Minimum, Optimum, Maximum Values

In justified type it is necessary to set a minimum word space value so that lines do not become too tight owing to too many characters being squeezed on to a line during justification.

It is also necessary to set a maximum value to avoid the development of loose lines. These are particularly common in column layouts where a line containing a single long word follows a line containing shorter words.

If hyphenation is not used, the long word may appear on a line by itself and the preceding line may contain only two or three words with very large gaps between them. In such a case it is likely that the maximum value has been exceeded and a loose line has developed. This can be overcome either by hyphenating the long word so that part of it drops back to the previous line, or by increasing letterspacing which has the effect of reducing word spacing.

If the combination of justification, your chosen column width, and your chosen typeface seems particularly prone to loose lines consider switching to ragged right alignment or change to a condensed typeface.

x-height

see also: point size, type size

The x-height of a typeface is defined as the height of a lowercase 'x' measured upwards from the baseline.

Different typefaces of the same point size may look large or small when visually compared. This is because their respective x-heights are different.

x-height can be a better practical measure of type size than point size. Differences can be considerable. For example, 10 point Bembo and 10 point Univers show a 2.5 point difference in x-height.

It is important to consider x-height when selecting a typeface for a job. When using a very small typeface, for example, it is better to use one with a large x-height to provide maximum legibility. Or, to look at it another way, using a small typeface with a large x-height means that you can fit more copy into the available space without compromising legibility. This can also be combined with reduced leading in proportion to the type size reduction thus saving even more space.

above: these examples clearly illustrate variation in x-height between various typefaces. The typefaces, from the left, are Helvetica, Letter Gothic, Palatino, and Goudy Old Style. All are 60 points in size.

Index